P9-DND-116

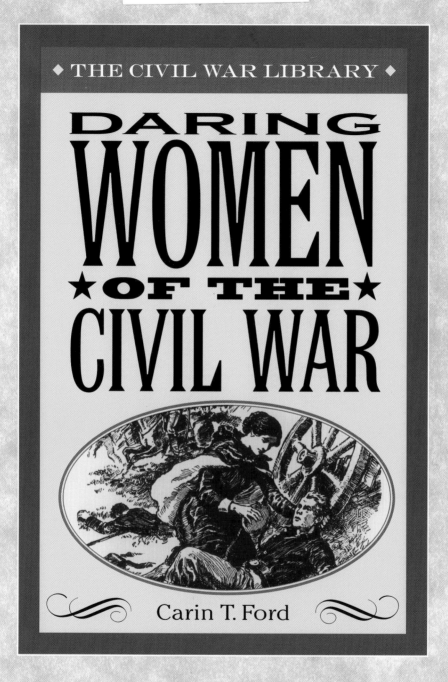

◆ THE CIVIL WAR LIBRARY ◆

DARING
WOMEN
★ OF THE ★
CIVIL WAR

Carin T. Ford

Enslow Publishers, Inc.

40 Industrial Road   PO Box 38
Box 398   Aldershot
Berkeley Heights, NJ 07922   Hants GU12 6BP
USA   UK

http://www.enslow.com

Library of Congress Cataloging-in-Publication Data

Ford, Carin T.
     Daring women of the Civil War / Carin T. Ford.
          p. cm. — (The Civil War library)
     Summary: An account of the many roles played by women in the American Civil War, both on the battlefield and at home, introducing specific women such as author Louisa May Alcott and Confederate spy Rose O'Neal Greenhow.
     Includes bibliographical references and index.
     ISBN 0-7660-2250-1 (hardcover)
     1. United States—History—Civil War, 1861–1865—Women—Juvenile literature. 2. United States—History—Civil War, 1861–1865—Participation, Female—Juvenile literature. 3. United States—History—Civil War, 1861–1865—Social aspects—Juvenile literature. [1. United States—History—Civil War, 1861–1865. 2. Women—History—19th century.] I. Title. II. Series.
     E628.F67   2004
     973.7'082—dc21   2003006479

Printed in the United States of America

10 9 8 7 6 5 4 3 2 1

To Our Readers: We have done our best to make sure all Internet Addresses in this book were active and appropriate when we went to press. However, the author and the publisher have no control over and assume no liability for the material available on those Internet sites or on other Web sites they may link to. Any comments or suggestions can be sent by e-mail to comments@enslow.com or to the address on the back cover.

Every effort has been made to locate all copyright holders of material used in this book. If any errors or omissions have occurred, corrections will be made in future editions of this book.

Illustration Credits: *American Advertising Posters of the Nineteenth Century*, Dover Publications, Inc., 1976, p. 6T; ArtToday.com, p. 19T; © Bettmann/Corbis, p. 28; Boston Public Library/Rare Books Department. Courtesy of the Trustees, pp. 29L, 29R; Collection of The New-York Historical Society, pp. 2, 25T, 30B; Courtesy Orchard House/The Louisa May Alcott Memorial Association, p. 6B; Courtesy State Archives of Michigan, p. 34R; *Frank Leslie's Illustrated Newspaper*, November 22, 1862, pp. 33 (inset), 34L; Library of Congress, pp. 1, 7, 8T, 8 (*Uncle Tom's Cabin*), 11 (background), 12L, 15T, 17, 18 (background), 19B, 20T, 20B, 22B, 23, 24T, 24C, 27 (inset/background), 30T, 32, 35L, 35R, 36, 37B, 38–39C, 38B, 39R, 40BC, 40–41T, 41T, 41TC, 41TR; Manuscripts, Archives & Rare Books Division, Schomburg Center for Research in Black Culture, The New York Public Library, Astor, Lenox and Tilden Foundations, pp. 24TR, 40–41B; The Museum of the Confederacy, Richmond, Virginia, Photography by Katherine Wetzel, pp. 5, 14, 18 (inset), 22T, 40TL; The Museum of the Confederacy, Richmond, Virginia, pp. 15 (socks), 26; National Archives and Records Administration, pp. 8 (Stowe), 21, 24TL, 25B, 31, 33 (background), 37T, 40TC; North Wind Picture Archives, pp. 4–5, 9, 10, 11 (inset), 13, 16; Western History/Genealogy Department, Denver Public Library, pp. 12R, 41BR.

Cover Illustrations: All cover photos courtesy of the following: Library of Congress; National Archives; Photos.com; Enslow Publishers, Inc.; with the exception of: Song Book, Courtesy National Park Service, Museum Management Program and Gettysburg National Military Park, catalog number GETT31374, www.cr.nps.gov/museum/exhibits/gettex/music2.htm; Patriotic Cover, Courtesy National Park Service, Museum Management Program and Gettysburg National Military Park, catalog number GETT27703, www.cr.nps.gov/museum/exhibits/gettex/write5.htm; Drum carried by Mozart Regiment, Courtesy National Park Service, Museum Management Program and Gettysburg National Military Park, catalog number GETT32847, www.cr.nps.gov/museum/exhibits/gettex/music3.htm; US Flag, Courtesy National Park Service, Museum Management Program and Manassas National Battlefield Park, catalog number MANA979, www.cr.nps.gov/museum/exhibits/flags/mana2.htm.

TABLE OF CONTENTS

CHAPTER ONE

WOMEN'S WORK

It was April 1861, and Louisa May Alcott wrote in her diary, "I long to be a man."[1]

The Civil War had just begun. Louisa was twenty-nine years old and wanted to be a soldier.

But Louisa could not join the army. She was a woman—and "women's work" was in the house. Their jobs were cooking, cleaning,

sewing, washing, and caring for children. Women's work did not include being a soldier.

There were many things that the laws of the United States did not allow women to do in the 1800s:

- ❖ They could not vote.
- ❖ They could not own property.
- ❖ They could not serve on a jury.
- ❖ They could not be elected to political office.

When the Civil War broke out, men had to leave their homes and jobs to become soldiers. Women suddenly found themselves taking on new roles and more responsibilities than they ever had before.

◆ LOUISA MAY ALCOTT (1832–1888) ◆

Louisa May Alcott was born in Germantown, Pennsylvania. She began writing at an early age and had some poetry and short stories published in popular magazines. In 1854 she wrote her first book, *Flower Fables*.

As a nurse in the Civil War, Alcott came down with typhoid fever after only six weeks on

the job. She was sent home. She based the book *Hospital Sketches* (published in 1863) on her time as a nurse.

When Alcott was in her mid-thirties, her publisher asked her to write a book for girls. The result was her most famous work, *Little Women*, a novel set in New England during the Civil War. Louisa went on to write more than thirty books.

hy was the United States being torn apart by war? The bad feelings between the North and South had started with slavery. Most Southerners were farmers, and their biggest crop was cotton. To produce millions of bales of cotton each year, the farmers needed plenty of field workers.

Their answer was African slaves—people who were kidnapped in Africa and brought to America in chains. Slaves did not have to be paid. They were property, bought and sold like animals. The owners, or masters, forced their slaves to work.

The businesses, factories, and small farms in the North did not need slaves. Also, most Northerners believed it was wrong for one person to own another. One by one, the states in the North put an end to slavery. Yet some Northerners wanted to see slavery stopped in the South, too.

When women first joined the struggle against slavery, they used the only weapon they had: their words.

THE FACTS ON:

ABOLITION

❖ People who wanted to abolish— or end—slavery were called abolitionists.

❖ They published newspapers against slavery and gave speeches about how badly slaves were treated.

In Harriet Beecher Stowe's book *Uncle Tom's Cabin*, a slave mother named Eliza flees across a frozen river to save her young child from slavery.

Angelina Grimké grew up in Charleston, South Carolina. Her family owned many slaves. As a teenager, Angelina saw a young slave whose master had whipped him so badly that the boy could hardly walk. Angelina knew this was not right.

When she was older, she and her sister, Sarah, left their home and headed North. There, the two women wrote newspaper articles and gave speeches against slavery. However, most Northerners did not care about slaves in the South, and they thought speaking in public was not ladylike. Crowds often made fun of the sisters and threw apples at them.[2]

One of the strongest voices against slavery was a runaway slave who called herself Sojourner Truth. She used her loud voice and sharp wit as weapons against

Isabella Baumfree changed her name to Sojourner Truth to show that she would always tell the truth.

8

slavery. Often, her audiences cried as she talked about the horrors that she and other slaves had suffered.

The woman with the most powerful words of all was Harriet Beecher Stowe. In 1851 Stowe started writing *Uncle Tom's Cabin*, about an old slave named Uncle Tom and his cruel master, Simon Legree. Reading this heartbreaking story made many Northerners more upset and angry about slavery than ever before.[3]

When Abraham Lincoln was elected president in 1860, many Southerners were afraid he would put an end to

Southerners said they needed slaves. Without slaves, farmers could not grow as much cotton—and less cotton meant less money for the farmer.

❖ Secede means "to break away." Eleven Southern states seceded from the United States.

❖ President Abraham Lincoln began fighting the Civil War because he did not want to let the United States split in two.

slavery. Seven Southern states broke away from the United States—South Carolina, Alabama, Florida, Mississippi, Louisiana, Texas, and Georgia. They formed their own country, the Confederate States of America. Lincoln wanted to keep the country united, and fighting broke out between the North and South. Soon, Virginia, Arkansas, Tennessee, and North Carolina joined the Confederacy.

Few people thought the Civil War would last long. But as the fighting dragged on for four bloody years, it became clear that more help was needed, both at home and on the battlefield.

On April 12, 1861, Confederate soldiers fired on Fort Sumter in Charleston, South Carolina. People watched the attack from rooftops. This was the start of the Civil War.

10

CHAPTER TWO

THE HOME FRONT

They are coming! The Yankees are coming at last!" wrote Sarah Morgan Dawson in her diary on March 14, 1863. Union troops were pushing their way toward her home in Louisiana. "For four or five hours the sound of their cannon has assailed our ears. There!—that one shook my bed!"[1]

❖ The North was also known as the Union, or the United States. The people there were often called Yankees.

❖ The South was called the Confederacy, or the Confederate States. During the war, Southerners were sometimes called Rebels or Johnny Reb.

Like countless other women in the North and South, Sarah kept a diary during the Civil War. For some women, writing helped pass the time. For nearly all, it was a way to express worries, hopes, and fears.

Mary Boykin Chesnut wrote the most famous diary of the war years. She filled fifty notebooks with more than 400,000 words. Mary was a wealthy Southerner whose family owned many slaves. She described the events of the war in great detail.

"At half-past four the heavy booming of a cannon," she wrote when the Confederate soldiers fired on Fort Sumter. "I sprang out of bed and on my knees . . . I prayed as I never prayed before."[2]

Many diaries, like the one written by Mary Chesnut, were later published. That is how we know what some women were thinking about, and doing, during the Civil War.

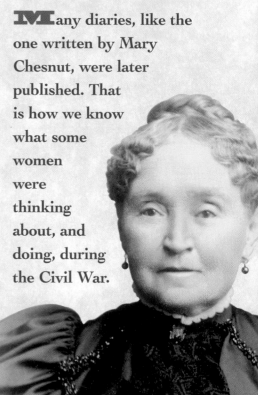

In the North, many of the women who kept diaries wrote about being wartime nurses and working to end slavery. Sophronia Bucklin described nursing the soldiers at a war hospital set up near the battlefield. Her diary was published as *In Hospital and Camp*. Laura Haviland of Michigan wrote *A Woman's Life-Work*. She told of her work on the Underground Railroad. This secret network of people and escape routes helped thousands of slaves run away to freedom. Twelve-

year-old Tillie Pierce Alleman wrote about seeing the Battle of Gettysburg in *At Gettysburg or What a Girl Saw and Heard of the Battle*.

Most women could not sit still during the war.

"Their cause is our cause," said one Georgia woman.

"We can work for those who go and [we can] pray . . ."[3]

Women were left to handle all of their household chores in addition to the men's work.

Sending
the men off
to war:
Women
helped
soldiers get
ready.

Many women joined soldiers' aid societies. These groups sewed soldiers' uniforms, hospital clothing, and bandages.

Women also put together small bags called comforts or hussies, which stood for "housewives."[4] They filled these bags for the soldiers with pins, needles, buttons, tape, quinine (a medicine), and other small goods.

Most battles of the Civil War were fought in the South. So the war had an even greater effect on the lives of Southern women. Their husbands, brothers, and sons had joined the Confederate army. Southern women had no choice but to take charge of their households.

In the towns, small farms, and large plantations of the South, women prepared food and cared for their children. But now they had to do the men's work, too.

14

They planted crops, plowed fields, cut firewood, and fed the animals. For many, this was the first time in their lives that they had ever worked so hard. "I find myself, every day, doing something I never did before," wrote Mary Lee of Virginia.[5]

Their work was made even more difficult by the North's

These Southern women spent many hours spinning, weaving, and sewing clothes for the Confederate soldiers.

Many women had never worked outside the home before. Here, they were making cartridges for the soldiers' guns.

wartime plan. Northern ships blocked Southern ports, so ships could not deliver their cargo of food, clothing, and other goods. The women of the South had to make shoes out of cloth or paper, twist rags into candles, and use berry juice as ink for their pens.

Women also spun thread on spinning wheels, then wove it into cloth on their looms. Many took up knitting and sewing.

They cut up their dresses to make flags and men's shirts. They trimmed their carpets into blankets. Countless hours were spent knitting mittens and socks for the soldiers. One South Carolina woman said, "We spent all our spare time knitting socks . . . and we never went out to pay a visit without taking our knitting along."[6]

In addition, businesses needed workers to replace the men off at war. Large numbers of women took jobs in offices. Others were hired by factories that made weapons and war goods. From 1860 to 1870, the number of women earning salaries more than doubled.[7]

In factories like these, many women in both the North and South were earning money for the first time in their lives.

CHAPTER THREE

SERVING AS NURSES

As soon as the Civil War began, hundreds of women on both sides wanted to be nurses in hospitals. They were quickly given the same answer: "It is no place for women."[1]

At that time, army hospitals had male nurses. Most were patients who had gotten better. These soldiers were often still weak from their wounds or illness—but at least they were men. In those days it was simply not considered proper for a woman to take care of a male stranger. Also, people thought women were too delicate for the shocking sights of death, disease, and crippled bodies.

In the early 1800s, women were thought of as weak and delicate. The large hoop skirts they wore made it impossible to bend at the waist. A woman could not even tie her shoe without help.

As the war went on, the number of wounded soldiers continued to grow. More help was desperately needed in the hospitals. At last, women were allowed to take part. Dorothea Dix was given the job of hiring and training nurses for the Union army. Nicknamed "Dragon Dix," she had spent more

◆ THE U.S. SANITARY COMMISSION ◆

The Sanitary Commission was founded in June 1861. Its goal was to take care of the soldiers' health by keeping the camps and hospitals clean (sanitary). With the help of hundreds of women, the Sanitary Commission collected food, clothing, and medical supplies for the soldiers. Workers also held bake sales and carnivals, called sanitary fairs. They raised millions of dollars for the war.

"God knows what we should have done without them," said Frederick Law Olmsted, secretary of the commission. "They have worked like heroes night and day."[2]

Workers brought relief wagons to the battlefield.

than twenty years working in mental hospitals and prisons.

Dix wanted to be sure that her female nurses were taken seriously. She hired only plain-looking women who were older than thirty. The nurses had to dress in brown or black. They could not wear bows, curls, jewelry, or fancy skirts.[3] Although Dix was strict, at least two thousand women went to work for her.

Many people in the hospitals still did not think women should be nurses. Georgeanna M. Woolsey, one of the first nurses to work in a Union army hospital, wrote, "Hardly a surgeon of whom I can think, received or treated [nurses] with even common courtesy."[4]

Like male nurses, most women had no training for the job. Still, they were able to help in a number of ways. "Till noon I trot, trot giving out

Some soldiers were cared for on the battlefield while others were carried off to hospitals.

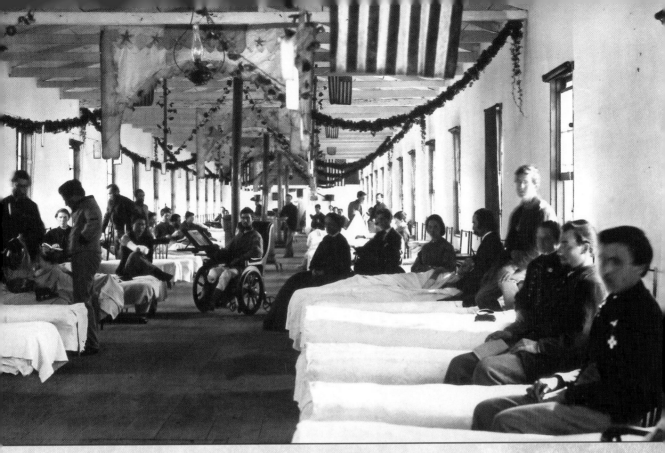

rations, cutting up food for helpless 'boys,' washing faces . . .
dressing wounds . . . dusting tables, sewing bandages, keeping
my tray tidy, rushing up & down with pillows, bed linen,
sponges, books & directions, till it seems as if I would joyfully
[give anything] for fifteen minutes rest," wrote Louisa May
Alcott.[5] She was helping out in a Union
hospital in Washington, D.C.

Nurses were not given much to eat,
and they often worked all night long with

Dorothea Dix was sickly, but she never missed a day of work.

Many army nurses died after catching such diseases as measles, typhoid, and smallpox from sick soldiers. The hospital above was in Washington, D.C.

Hospitals were set up right at the battlefields.

no rest. Sometimes the only place they could sleep was on the floor, their clothing splattered with blood from the wounded soldiers.

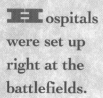

In the hospitals set up near battlefields, the job was even harder. Nurses could be called to work at any time of the day or night. They were tired all the time and often slept on the cold ground. Their hands swelled, and their feet blistered. They could be killed by nearby gunfire.

Still, the work went on.

Clara Barton was known as the "Angel of the Battlefield."[6] At the start of the war, she worked in a government office in Washington, D.C. When she learned that hundreds of wounded soldiers needed medical supplies, Barton jumped into action. She put ads in newspapers to gather what was needed. Then she came up with a plan to bring the supplies to the soldiers.

Traveling into the war area with mules and wagons, Barton said, "I went in while the battle raged."[7] She would later go on to set up the American Red Cross. Today this organization continues to help sick and wounded people during wars, floods, and other disasters.

Mary Ann "Mother" Bickerdyke traveled to nineteen battlefields during the four years of the Civil War. She cleaned hospital buildings for the Union army and ordered bathtubs to be made from barrels. She set up kitchens to make sure the soldiers ate healthy foods. If she saw dishonest or lazy

Clara Barton often stayed with the wounded men until they could be carried to safety. Here, she was giving a wounded soldier a drink.

Left: After the war, Clara Barton set up an office to search for missing soldiers.

Center: Mother Bickerdyke ordered everybody around—even the officers.

Right: Susie King Taylor was one of the first African-American nurses in United States history.

workers, she had them fired from their jobs. Often she walked about the battlefields at night with a lantern, searching for wounded soldiers.

Susie King Taylor was a runaway slave from Georgia. During the Civil War, she worked as a laundress and nurse in an African-American regiment of the Union army. Taylor also taught the soldiers to read and write. She had learned these skills from her master's daughter.[8]

In the South, most hospitals would not allow women to care for wounded soldiers. Yet many Confederate women simply took matters into their own hands. During the first Battle of Bull Run, women from Virginia came to the battlefield and took care of injured soldiers throughout the day and night.[9]

In cities such as Atlanta, Georgia, and Chattanooga, Tennessee, private homes were set up to offer food, shelter, and rest to sick soldiers.[10]

In this letter, a nurse tells her family about the war.

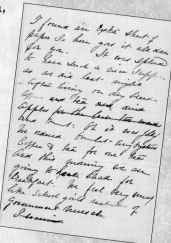

Sally Tomkins used her own money to turn her friend's Richmond, Virginia, home into a hospital. There, Tomkins cared for more than a thousand wounded soldiers. She was the only woman to be made an officer in the Confederate army.

Juliet Opie Hopkins also spent her money and time in Richmond hospitals. She took charge of caring for wounded

◆ DR. MARY EDWARDS WALKER ◆

Very few women in the United States were doctors in the mid-1800s. Dr. Mary Edwards Walker wanted to be a surgeon for the Union army, but she was turned down. Walker did not give up. Wearing pants, suspenders, and a knee-length dress, she volunteered her skills in a hospital in Washington, D.C. She wrote that her patients were "very much pleased" to see her—even if the male doctors were not.[11] Near the end of the war, Walker was finally hired as an army surgeon. She was the only woman in the war to be awarded the Congressional Medal of Honor. This is the highest honor given to a citizen of the United States.

soldiers from Alabama. In thanks for her work, Alabama lawmakers printed Hopkins's picture on its state money.

Kate Cumming, also of Alabama, helped nurse Confederate soldiers in a Mississippi hotel that was turned into a hospital. In April 1862, Cumming wrote in her diary that wounded soldiers were lying "so close together that it was almost impossible to walk without stepping on them. . . . I sat up all night, bathing the men's wounds, and giving them water.[12]

The work was difficult, but the women did not give up. They kept the hospitals clean and organized, and they took good care of the soldiers. In addition, women cheered up their patients by singing in the wards, writing letters for the soldiers, and hanging bright curtains from the hospital windows.[13]

The work of these female nurses made a big difference. One study of hospitals reported that the patients were better off when female nurses cared for them. Twice as many patients died under the care of male nurses.[14]

CHAPTER FOUR

FIGHTING AS SOLDIERS

In the spring of 1864, Private Lyons Wakeman fell ill and was sent to a hospital in New Orleans, Louisiana. About six weeks later, the soldier died. There was nothing unusual about Wakeman's death. For every soldier killed in battle during the war, two others died from disease.[1]

But Private Wakeman was different from the other soldiers. "He" was a woman.

At least four hundred women disguised themselves as men and fought in the Civil War. Some women joined the army because they did not want to be parted from their husbands. Some wanted to serve their country. Others were just looking for adventure.

Nineteen-year-old Sarah Rosetta Wakeman was tired of staying home on the family farm. So she gave her name as "Lyons," claimed she was twenty-one, and joined the army. "I [am] enjoying my Self better this summer than I ever did before in this world," she wrote to her family in June 1863. "I have good Clothing and enough to eat and nothing to do, only to handle my gun and that I can do as well as the rest of them."[2]

In the army, Loreta Janeta Velazquez even learned to smoke cigars like a man.

Women were not allowed to become soldiers, so they had to pretend to be men. They wore men's clothing, cut their hair short, and used men's names.

Loreta Janeta Velazquez had been interested in war since she was a child. In the Civil War she fought for the Confederacy under the name Harry Buford. "Braiding my hair very close, I put on a man's wig, and a false mustache, and by tucking my pantaloons in my boots . . . I managed to transform myself into a very presentable man," she wrote.[3]

Lucinda Horne traveled with the 14th South Carolina Volunteer Infantry. She was present at nine battles, including the Battle of Gettysburg, right. She nursed the wounded soldiers on the battlefields.

Female soldiers not only needed to look like men, they needed to *act* like men, too. They learned to drink, smoke, and chew tobacco, like the other soldiers. When they were wounded, female soldiers often refused medical care. They did not want to take off their clothing.

In 1863 one Indiana cavalryman wrote: "We discovered

◆ FOLLOWING THE TROOPS ◆

Not all women who followed the troops served as nurses or soldiers. Some were soldiers' wives, girlfriends, or relatives, as well as laundresses.

Vivandières (which means "hospitality givers") and the Daughters of the Regiment also traveled with the soldiers. They took part in parades and drills and often got a taste of battle. They carried water for the wounded soldiers, did laundry, and waved the company flag. These women usually wore sashes and lively uniforms. August Foster was a Daughter of the Regiment with the Second Maine Infantry. She spent most of her time nursing wounded soldiers. At Bull Run, she had her horse shot out from under her.

last week a soldier who turned out to be a girl. She had already been in service for twenty-one months and was twice wounded. Maybe she would have remained undiscovered for a long time if she hadn't fainted. She was given a warm bath which gave the secret away."[4]

Amy Clarke used the name "Richard Anderson" to join a Tennessee unit of the Confederacy. Fighting alongside her husband, she buried him on the battlefield at Shiloh. Clarke continued fighting until she was wounded in her ankle and chest. She was captured by Union soldiers and sent back to the Confederates—in a dress.

Jennie Hodgers joined the Union army in Illinois in 1862. The nineteen-year-old called herself Albert Cashier and fought in several battles, including the Battle of Vicksburg. After serving three years in the war, Hodgers kept up the disguise. Her true identity was

Mary Tipee served the troops as a *vivandière.*

✥ In daily army life, undressing was not usually a problem for women. Soldiers were always on the move. They could go for weeks without changing their clothes. For bathing, soldiers had time to wash only their faces and hands.

✥ Many women would move to another unit if they were in danger of being found out. Elizabeth Compton spent eighteen months in seven different units. Frances Hook served in units in Illinois, Michigan, and Tennessee.

discovered in 1911 when she broke her leg in a car accident. A doctor discovered that his patient was a woman, but he agreed to keep her secret.

Soldiers stood guard in all weather, marched for countless miles, and fought on the battlefield. A soldier's life was not easy. But for several hundred women—most of whose names will never even be known—the decision to join the army was the right one.

"The weather is cold and the ground is froze hard, but I sleep as warm in the tents as I would in a good bed," wrote Sarah Rosetta Wakeman in December 1862. "I like to be a soldier very well."[5]

Kady Brownell was the wife of an orderly sergeant in the First and Fifth Rhode Island Infantry. Wearing a short skirt over pants and a bright red sash, Brownell was the official company flagbearer.

CHAPTER FIVE

BECOMING SPIES

A group of slaves was building a fort for the Confederate army. They were using pickaxes, shovels, and wheelbarrows. The work was hot and sweaty. Suddenly, one slave pointed at another, saying that the man seemed to be "turning white."[1]

The "slave" who was turning white was

Some women smuggled important goods such as guns and medicine across enemy lines. They would often hide pistols and the medicine quinine in the false bottoms of trunks, as well as in their parasols and big hoop skirts.

really Sarah Emma Edmonds. She had fought for the Union under the name Frank Thompson. Now she was a spy. Wearing a dark wool wig, Edmonds was a white woman whose black makeup was fading as she sweated in the hot sun.

Edmonds worked among the Confederate soldiers and listened to their battle plans. When night came, she slipped

Edmonds later wrote a book about her days as a Union spy. She exaggerated some of her stories to make them more exciting.

away to deliver the information to the Union army. She was one of dozens of women in the North and South who risked their lives to spy on the enemy.

Mary Elizabeth Bowser was an ex-slave who spied for the Union. She worked for her former owner, Elizabeth Van Lew. Van Lew was known as "Crazy Bet."[2] She purposely acted odd so people would not suspect her of running a spy ring.

Bowser worked as a servant in the home of Jefferson Davis. He was the president of the Confederate States. Bowser listened closely to Davis's conversations with his dinner guests. She also looked at telegrams and important papers lying around the house. Everyone thought Bowser could not read, so these papers were not hidden away.

Elizabeth Van Lew had a secret room in her house to hide men who escaped from Confederate prisons.

Each night Bowser returned home to tell Van Lew what she had learned. Van Lew wrote everything down and hid the papers in the soles of boots or inside eggshells. Sometimes her notes were baked into loaves of bread. Then the hidden messages were delivered to the Union army.

Harriet Tubman asked other ex-slaves to help her spy for the Union army.

Like Bowser, Harriet Tubman was a former slave who spied for the Union. Through the years, she led more than three hundred slaves to freedom on the Underground

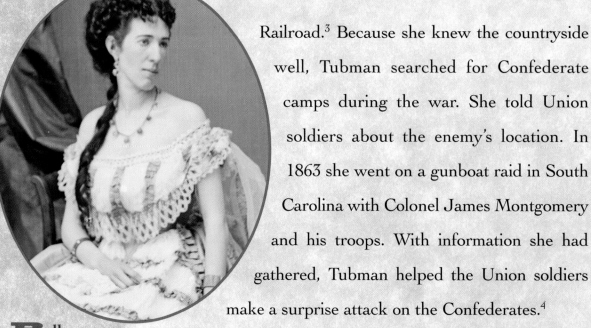

Railroad.[3] Because she knew the countryside well, Tubman searched for Confederate camps during the war. She told Union soldiers about the enemy's location. In 1863 she went on a gunboat raid in South Carolina with Colonel James Montgomery and his troops. With information she had gathered, Tubman helped the Union soldiers make a surprise attack on the Confederates.[4]

Belle Boyd seemed fearless. She was arrested as a spy and put in prison. As soon as she got out, she went right back to spying.

Actress Pauline Cushman performed shows for the Confederate army. Whenever she heard soldiers talking about war plans, she secretly sent the information to Union officers. When Cushman was caught, she was sentenced to death by hanging. But the Union army captured the town, and Cushman was freed. She returned to acting after the war.

Belle Boyd of West Virginia worked for the Confederacy. A young woman with a great deal of charm, Boyd made friends with Union soldiers. Then she passed along information about battle plans to the Confederate generals.

One time, Union officers were meeting at a room in her aunt's home. Boyd knew about a closet upstairs with a hole in the floor. Boyd wrote, "I stole softly upstairs, and, lying on the floor of the closet, applied my ear to the hole, and found, to my great joy, I could distinctly hear the conversation that was passing below."[5]

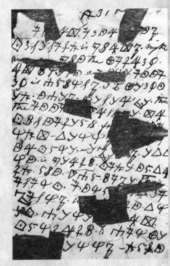

This is one of the coded messages that Rose O'Neal Greenhow sent to Confederate leaders.

Boyd wrote the information in code and brought it to the Confederate army. After the war Boyd went onstage, doing shows about her life as a spy.

A rich widow in her forties, Rose O'Neal Greenhow gave many parties for important people in Washington, D.C. She was also a Confederate spy. In talking to Union army officers, she learned how many soldiers, and which roads, the Union planned to use in their attack on

Rose O'Neal Greenhow's daughter came to visit her in prison.

Manassas, Virginia, in 1861. She sent a coded message with her friend, who was disguised as a farm girl. Greenhow's friend carried the note in a bun in her hair. Some historians give Greenhow part of the credit for the Confederate victory at the first Battle of Bull Run.

Although many female spies were caught and put in prison, some worked throughout the war

Greenhow warned the Confederates of the Union army's plan to attack in the first Battle of Bull Run.

without being discovered. Yet all were willing to give their lives for what they believed in. Written on the grave of Elizabeth Van Lew are the words: "She risked everything that is dear to man—friends, fortune, comfort, health, life itself."[6]

~⟋

After the Civil War ended, many women wanted to continue in the new roles they had taken on during the past four years. But the husbands, brothers, and sons who returned home took charge once again. Women went back to the work they had done before the war.

The soldiers came home, and women went back to "women's work." But the war had shown women that they could do more.

Still, everything was not the same. Women had proved that they were very capable of doing "men's work." Over time, their voices would grow louder and stronger in demanding to be treated equally.

DARING WOMEN OF THE ★ CIVIL WAR ★ TIMELINE

1860
Abraham Lincoln is elected president of the United States.

1861
Six more Southern states secede, and the Confederate States of America is formed, with Jefferson Davis as president.

Shots are fired at Fort Sumter, and the Civil War begins.

1861
The United States Sanitary Commission is set up to provide care for wounded soldiers.

Clara Barton brings supplies to the Union army.

Pre–1860s	1860	1861

1835
Angelina Grimké joins the abolitionist movement.

1843
Isabella Baumfree changes her name to Sojourner Truth and begins speaking out against slavery.

1850
Harriet Tubman makes the first of nineteen trips south on the Underground Railroad.

1851
Harriet Beecher Stowe's *Uncle Tom's Cabin* appears in newspapers as a weekly series.

1860
South Carolina secedes from the United States.

1861
Four more Southern states secede.

Dorothea Dix is put in charge of all women nurses working in Union hospitals.

DOROTHEA DIX

1861
Harriet Tubman begins spying for the Union army.

Rose O'Neal Greenhow's spying helps the Confederates win the first Battle of Bull Run.

1863
Lincoln issues the Emancipation Proclamation.

1862
Susie King Taylor begins as a laundress and then becomes a nurse for the Union.

1863
The Union wins the Battle of Gettysburg, and President Lincoln gives the Gettysburg Address.

1864
Ulysses S. Grant is named commander of the Union army.

1865
Confederate general Robert E. Lee surrenders to Union general Ulysses S. Grant.

President Lincoln is assassinated. Andrew Johnson becomes president.

1862 **1863** **1864** **1865**

SUSIE KING TAYLOR

1863
Louisa May Alcott publishes *Hospital Sketches*, which tells of her experiences as a war nurse in Washington, D.C.

1863
Harriet Tubman assists Colonel James Montgomery as a scout on a gunboat raid in South Carolina.

1864
Lincoln is elected to a second term as president.

MARY CHESNUT

1865
The Thirteenth Amendment to the Constitution abolishes slavery in the United States.

Dr. Mary Edwards Walker receives Congressional Medal of Honor.

❧ Words to Know ❧

abolish — To end; to get rid of.

Amendment — A change made to the U.S. Constitution.

cavalry — Soldiers who fight on horseback.

civil war — A war between people of the same country.

Confederate States of America — The new nation formed by eleven Southern states that seceded from the United States of America: South Carolina, Mississippi, Florida, Alabama, Georgia, Louisiana, Texas, Virginia, Arkansas, North Carolina, and Tennessee. Also called the Confederacy.

emancipation — Setting someone free.

enlist — To enroll in the military.

hoop skirt — A woman's skirt with a large, flexible circle placed at the bottom to make it puff out.

Words to Know

indentured servant — A person who must work as a servant for several years before being given his or her freedom.

infantry — Soldiers who are trained to fight on foot.

plantation — A large farm.

quinine — A bitter substance that comes from the bark of the cinchona tree and is used in medicine.

secede — To withdraw from a group.

surgeon — A doctor who performs operations.

Underground Railroad — A secret network of escape routes and people who helped slaves run away to freedom.

Union — The Northern states that remained under the United States government during the Civil War.

Chapter Notes

CHAPTER 1.
Women's Work

1. Joel Myerson and Daniel Shealy, eds., *The Journals of Louisa May Alcott* (Boston: Little, Brown, and Company, 1989), p. 105.
2. "The Legendary Ladies of the Civil War," *Civil War Women . . . They Ain't No Scarlett O'Hara*, 2001, <http://www.civilwarwomen. homestead.com> (June 12, 2003).
3. Geoffrey C. Ward, *The Civil War: An Illustrated History* (New York: Knopf, 1990), p. 19.

CHAPTER 2.
The Home Front

1. Sarah Morgan Dawson, *A Confederate Girl's Diary* (Athens, Ga.: University of Georgia Press, 1991), p. 438.
2. Mary Boykin Chesnut, *A Diary from Dixie* (Chapel Hill, N.C.: University of North Carolina Press, 1997), p. 35.
3. William C. Davis, *Look Away! A History of the Confederate States of America* (New York: The Free Press, 2002), p. 194.
4. Agatha Young, *Women and the Crisis: Women of the North in the Civil War* (New York: McDowell, Obolensky, 1959), p. 69.
5. Drew Gilpin Faust, *Mothers of Invention: Women of the Slaveholding South in the Civil War* (Chapel Hill, N.C.: The University of North Carolina Press, 1996), p. 49.
6. Bell Irvin Wiley, *Confederate Women*. (New York: Barnes and Noble Books, 1975). p. 145.

7. Mary Elizabeth Massey, *Bonnet Brigades* (New York: Alfred A. Knopf, 1966), p. 151.

CHAPTER 3.
Serving as Nurses

1. Sylvia Dannett, *Noble Women of the North* (New York: T. Yoseloff, 1959), p. 68.
2. Mary Elizabeth Massey, *Bonnet Brigades* (New York: Alfred A. Knopf, 1966), p. 54.
3. Agatha Young, *The Women and the Crisis* (New York: McDowell, Obolensky, 1959), p. 98.
4. Mary P. Ryan, *Womanhood in America: From Colonial Times to the Present* (New York: New Viewpoints, 1975; new edition, 1983), p. 200.
5. Joel Myerson and Daniel Shealy, eds., *The Journals of Louisa May Alcott* (Boston: Little, Brown, and Company, 1989), p. 114.
6. *Life Stories of Civil War Heroes, 2001–2003* <http://www.geocities.com/Athens/Aegean/6732/cb.html> (June 12, 2003).
7. "Civil War Nurses, Angels of the Battlefield," *Shotgun's Home of the American Civil War* <http://www.civilwarhome.com/civilwarnurses.htm> (June 12, 2003).
8. Charles H. Wesley and Patricia W. Romero, *Negro Americans in the Civil War: From Slavery to Citizenship* (New York: Publishers Company, Inc., 1967), p. 108.
9. Davis, p. 195.

10. Bell Irvin Wiley, *Confederate Women* (New York: Barnes and Noble Books, 1975), p. 144.

11. Elizabeth D. Leonard, *Yankee Women: Gender Battles in the Civil War* (New York: W.W. Norton & Company, 1994), p. 117.

12. Katharine M. Jones, *Heroines of Dixie* (New York: Konecky & Konecky, 1955), p. 109.

13. George Worthington Adams, *Doctors in Blue: The Medical History of the Union Army in the Civil War* (Baton Rouge, La.: Louisiana State University Press, 1952), p. 163.

14. Drew Gilpin Faust, *Mothers of Invention: Women of the Slaveholding South in the Civil War* (Chapel Hill: The University of North Carolina Press, 1996), p. 97.

CHAPTER 4.
Fighting as Soldiers

1. Shelby Foote, *The Civil War: A Narrative, Red River to Appomattox* (New York: Random House, 1974), vol. 3, p. 1040.

2. Lauren Cook Burgess, *An Uncommon Soldier* (Pasadena, Md.: The Minerva Center, 1994), p. 31.

3. Loreta Janeta Velazquez, *The Woman in Battle: A Narrative of the Exploits, Adventures, and Travels of Madame Loreta Janeta Velaquez* (Richondz: Dustin, Gilman & Co., 1876), p. 53.

4. Wendy A. King, *Clad in Uniform: Women Soldiers of the Civil War*, <http://www.geocities.com/womansoldier/womenofficers.html> (June 12, 2003).

5. Burgess, p. 21–22.

CHAPTER 5.
Becoming Spies

1. Sarah Emma Edmonds, "Spies, Raiders & Partisans," *The War for States' Rights*, <http://civilwar.bluegrass.net/SpiesRaidersAndPartisans/sarahemmaedmonds.html> (June 12, 2003).

2. Mary Elizabeth Massey, *Bonnet Brigades* (New York: Alfred A. Knopf, 1966), p. 101.

3. Lerone Bennett, Jr., *Before the Mayflower: A History of Black America* (Chicago: Johnson Publishing Company, Inc., 1969), p. 146.

4. Agatha Young, *The Women and the Crisis* (New York: McDowell, Obolensky, 1959), p. 303.

5. Belle Boyd, *Belle Boyd in Camp and Prison* (London: Saunders, Otley, and Co., 1865), p. 106.

6. Massey, p. 87.

∽ Learn More ∽

Caravantes, Peggy. *Petticoat Spies: Six Women Spies of the Civil War*. Greensboro, N.C.: Morgan Reynolds, 2002.

Chang, Ina. *A Separate Battle: Women and the Civil War*. New York: Lodestar Books, 1991.

Furbee, Mary Rodd. *Outrageous Women of Civil War Times*. Hoboken, N.J.: John Wiley, 2003.

Helletly, LeeAnne. *Harriet Beecher Stowe: Author of Uncle Tom's Cabin*. Broomall, Pa.: Chelsea House Publishers, 2000.

Savage, Douglas J. *Women in the Civil War*. Philadelphia: Chelsea House Publishers, 2000.

Zeinert, Karen. *Those Courageous Women of the Civil War*. Brookfield, Conn.: Millbrook Press, 1998.

Internet Addresses

"Civil War Women." Online Archival Collections, Special Collections Library, Duke University
    <http://odyssey.lib.duke.edu/collections/civil-war-women.html>

"Hearts at Home: Southern Women in the Civil War"
    <http://www.lib.virginia.edu/speccol/exhibits/hearts/>

"Civil War Women: Primary Sources on the Internet"
    <http://scriptorium.lib.duke.edu/women/cwdocs.html>

Index

Pages numbers for photographs are in **boldface** type.